Everything You Need To Know

WHEN A PARENT IS OUT OF WORK

Going through the newspaper's daily want ads can be a tiring and frustrating task for an out-of-work parent.

• THE NEED TO KNOW LIBRARY •

Everything You Need To Know

WHEN A PARENT IS OUT OF WORK

Stephanie St. Pierre

Series Editor: Evan Stark, Ph.D.

THE ROSEN PUBLISHING GROUP, INC.
NEW YORK

Published in 1991 by The Rosen Publishing Group, Inc.
29 East 21st Street, New York, New York 10010

First Edition
Copyright © 1991 by The Rosen Publishing Group, Inc.

Manufactured in the United States of America.

Library of Congress Cataloging-in-Publication Data

St. Pierre, Stephanie.
    Everything you need to know when a parent is out of work/
Stephanie St. Pierre.— 1st ed.
    (Need to know library)
    Includes bibliographical references and index.
    Summary: Readers learn about some of the reasons that can cause a
parent to lose his or her job, and how to help their families cope with
change and the possibility of hard times.
    ISBN 0-8239-1217-6
    1. Unemployment—Social aspects—Juvenile literature. 2. Parent
and child—Juvenile literature. 3. Work and family—Juvenile literature. [1. Unemployment.] I. Title. II. Series.
HO8708.S7 1991
331.137—dc20   90-26487
                                                                                              CIP
                                                                                              AC

Contents

Introduction

Most people are unemployed (out of work) at least once or twice in their working lives. People become unemployed for many reasons. Some people cannot work because they are injured. Sometimes a company goes out of business. Sometimes people leave one job to look for a better one. Or a parent may be fired for not doing a job properly. Whenever a parent is out of work, it is a hard time for him or her, and for the family.

A parent who is out of work may feel depressed. In fact, a parent may be too embarrassed to say he or she is out of a job. It can be very scary to find out that your parent is out of work. Maybe you haven't been told by your parent. It can be confusing and upsetting to find out some other way.

Some parents don't think their children should be told about the unemployment. They don't want their children to worry. Other parents share the information with the whole family. In fact, they may ask for advice from the family before they make a job change.

You may have to face some hard changes when a parent is out of work. There will be a lot less money to meet family expenses. Your parents may worry a great deal. They may argue with each other.

If your parent is out of work for a very long time, your family may need help to pay bills. You may have to move to a cheaper apartment or house.

This book can help you understand your parent who is out of work. It can also help you to prepare for some of the things that may happen in your family. You are not responsible for finding your parent another job. It is not your job to work to support your family. But there are many ways that you can help your family through this hard time. This book will help you do that.

Workers who are part of a union may go on strike for higher wages, better working conditions, increased benefits, or other changes.

Chapter 1

Why Is Your Parent Out of Work?

People leave their jobs for many reasons. Some people lose their jobs. Some people quit. Some people are fired. Some reasons have nothing to do with how well a person can do his or her job.

Lay offs

Josie knew right away that something had happened. She was dressed for school and ready for a quick breakfast. Her father was sitting at the kitchen table drinking coffee.

Josie's father worked the early shift at a truck factory. He was always at work when she got up. This morning he was still at home. And he looked upset. Josie's father had been laid off.

9

Lay offs are a common reason that people are forced out of work. A person is laid off because an employer has a problem. If a factory can't sell the products it makes, it may go out of business. The people who work in the factory may be very good workers. But if the factory closes, they lose their jobs. They are laid off.

Sometimes people are laid off when a company has problems but it is not going out of business. By laying off some employees (workers), the company can continue to operate. It will be able to pay the rest of the employees.

Another reason for lay offs is changes in technology (the way things are done). New ways of doing things may put people out of work. A robot may weld rivets better and faster than any human can. Putting in a computer system may mean that an office only needs one secretary or file clerk. In these cases the workers who are no longer needed might be laid off.

Some jobs are needed only for certain seasons. In other seasons the workers are laid off. Agriculture (farming) is a good example. Many people may be needed to harvest a crop of lettuce, or cherries, or beans. But when the harvest is over, the workers are laid off.

There is an important difference between getting fired and being laid off. When a worker is laid off, it isn't his or her fault. Being laid off should not make it harder to get another job. A laid-off worker will not be blamed for being out of work.

Sometimes companies help workers who are laid off. They may continue to pay workers for some weeks or months after their jobs end. Or the company helps the workers find new jobs. But people who are laid off are not always treated well. Some lay offs are very sudden. A worker laid off with very little notice—or none at all—may feel upset.

If a person enjoyed his or her job very much, he or she will be very sad to be laid off. It may be hard to find a new job like the old one. Lay offs often happen when an industry is failing. It can be very hard for a laid-off worker to find the same kind of job. If the whole steel-making business is not doing well, there will be many lay offs. And there will be few if any new jobs. Most steel workers who are laid off will have to learn new jobs.

If your parent is laid off, how he or she feels about it will depend on why it happened. Those feelings will also depend on how difficult he or she thinks it will be to get another job.

Strikes

When a group of people leaves the workplace together, that is called a *strike*. Most strikes are organized (run) by unions. Unions are groups of working people that get together to make things better for everyone in the group. People go on strike for many reasons—to get better pay, or to refuse to work in unhealthy or unsafe conditions, for example. Striking is not quitting. When the strike ends, everyone goes back to work. If the strike is successful, everyone's job conditions will be better.

A strike can end after a few hours. Or a strike can last for many months. While a person is on strike, he or she may find another job that lasts for just a short time. But usually the striking group—the union—tries to help the workers support their families. Sometimes a union puts money aside. That money is called a "strike fund." Workers on strike can get money from the fund for rent, food, and other family expenses.

Disability

Sometimes people lose their jobs because they are not able to do them. A person who is sick or hurt and cannot continue to work is *disabled*. A lumberjack could not continue to work if his or her back was injured. It would not be possible to do hard

A disability caused by an accident or illness may mean a parent is out of work for a long time.

physical labor. A person who is very sick for a long time will need time to get back to work. He or she may be too weak to travel to work and put in a full day, even after getting well.

If a person is injured (hurt) on the job, his or her employer may give help. The company will help the worker find a new job or learn new skills. A person who is injured away from work, or becomes ill, will probably not receive such help.

Some people have disability insurance. If they are injured or ill and unable to work, they will be paid by the insurance company. The checks will not be as much as paychecks. But they will be sent like paychecks. The person will be paid for as long as he or she cannot work.

Disabilities can last a long time or a short time. They can keep a person out of work for weeks or months. A disabled person may have to find a whole new line of work.

Fired for Cause

Being "fired for cause" is probably the most up-setting way to lose a job. A worker is told to leave his or her job because the employer is not satisfied.

Some reasons a person might be fired are:
- being late many times
- incompetence (not doing a good job)

- drug or alcohol abuse
- not getting along with other workers
- stealing from the company

People are sometimes warned before they are fired. Then if they do not do better they are fired.

A person who is fired for cause may also be in trouble with the law. If someone is fired for stealing, the company may call the police. The employee may be arrested and tried in the courts for the crime.

Being fired for cause doesn't always mean a worker has done something wrong. Sometimes an employer unfairly accuses a worker of bad work habits or of doing a poor job. A person who did a perfectly good job may be fired. Perhaps she or he didn't fit in, or was not getting along with others who are important.

A good worker may also see something bad going on in the workplace. Fellow workers may be cheating the company, or stealing. If the boss, or supervisor, is part of what is going on, a worker who tells the supervisor may be fired. The worker "knows too much."

Losing a job under these circumstances is very difficult. When you are looking for a new job, it is hard to explain what happened. If a worker has been fired, he or she may not be able to get unemployment benefits (payments from the government

to aid people who are out of work) or other help.
A person who has lost his or her job will probably
suffer, even if the firing wasn't fair.

Quitting

Not everyone who is unemployed was forced out
of work. Some people choose to leave their jobs.

If a person is not getting ahead in a job because of
discrimination, for example, he or she might quit.
When a person is not given fair treatment because
of his or her race, or sex, or religion, that is discrimination. Discrimination is against the law, but it
still happens. It can make a job so terrible that a
person would rather be out of work. People can
fight discrimination in the courts, but it can take a
very long time. A worker who has been discriminated against will probably have to find another job.

*Keesha's mom was at home when she got back from
band practice. The smell of fresh-baked cookies filled
the house. Keesha had almost forgotten what having
her mom at home was like. Her mom had worked
full-time since Keesha was in the third grade. But
her mom was in college now. She'd left her job to go
back to school. And she was able to spend a lot more
time at home.*

*The family had talked about her mom's going back
to school. Keesha and her two brothers understood
that there would be less money for movies and pizza
for a while.*

Keesha's mom had been a waitress. Now she was going to be a nurse. When she went back to work, Keesha's mom would be able to make a lot more money.

Probably the best reason to leave a job is to take a better job. Sometimes a person can afford to leave his or her job and take time to look for a new and better one. Some people do this to start a new career. They may even go back to school to learn new things before they start to look.

Many people try to find better jobs while they are still employed. But this is not always possible. It may be a risk to quit a job to look for a better one. But sometimes that is the best thing a person can do.

Knowing the Reason Helps

It is very important to understand the reason why your parent is out of work. Then you will understand how long it may take him or her to get a new job. You will accept family changes more easily.

There are some things that will probably happen no matter what the reason is. You should be prepared for these things, so that you won't be worried or surprised. Most people who are out of work do not stay unemployed for more than a few months. Many times they go back to work much sooner.

The Unemployment Office temporarily pays cash benefits to any taxpayer who has lost a job.

Chapter 2

Immediate Effects on the Family

*S*andy's mom was still in her bathrobe when Sandy got home from school. This was the third day in a row that Sandy's mom hadn't left the house all day. Sandy was getting worried.

"Hi, Mom. How was your day?" Sandy asked cheerfully. Her mom didn't answer.

"Mom, are you okay?" Her mom looked up at her. "Oh, it's you. Is school over already?"

"What's for dinner, Mom? Can I help you with anything?"

Sandy's mom had lost her job as a switchboard operator. The company had a new system now that one of the secretaries could handle and still do her job. Sandy's mom missed the office, and the friends she had worked with. She didn't have any other office skills. And she was afraid that she would not be able to find work. She had been home for a month. Sandy was very worried about her.

Your parent is out of work. How will this affect the family? Even being out of work for a short time can be very upsetting. Here are some of the things that may happen in your family shortly after a parent stops working.

Stress

Stress is a word that means many different things. Stress is not always bad. Any change can bring stress and pressure. Along with change comes the need to act in new and different ways.

The changes that occur when a parent is out of work bring stress to the whole family. Even if the parent chose to leave a job to make a change for the better—like going back to school—it can be hard. An out-of-work parent may have a completely different schedule than in the past. He or she may be spending a lot of time at home. That can be nice if the parent is able to enjoy the time with the family. Still, the family routine will change. Your parent may be very unhappy about his or her situation. That can be difficult for everyone. You may wish he or she were not around so much.

When one parent is not working, the other may have to work much longer hours. The other parent may have to look for a job, even if he or she has never worked outside the home before. That is also a stress on the family. Everyone may have to take on new responsibilities. Children may have to be more helpful with household chores.

The stress of being out of work can cause some parents to overreact to small problems and accidents.

There is probably a lot of stress on you and your family when your parent is out of work. It can make you feel very worried, or tired, or angry, or sad, or just confused. It is very important to find healthy ways to deal with stress. We will cover some ways to do that in Chapter Four.

Depression

Everyone feels depressed at one time or another. Losing a job usually makes a person feel depressed for a little while. Feeling depressed is like feeling very, very sad. When someone is depressed, he or she may not want to eat, or sleep, or talk with friends. Some people eat too much when they are depressed. Some people sleep all day long. Some people get very cranky and seem to fight with everyone. Depression is different for everyone. Some people, when they are depressed, do things to try to feel better that don't really help. They may drink too much, or fight, or cry all the time.

Anyone who has lost his or her job will probably feel depressed for at least a short time. There are many reasons why. Sometimes people miss their old job and their friends at work. Some people feel that they have hurt the family by losing their job. A person may lose a job because of a disability. That person may worry about never being able to work again. Sometimes a person is fired for doing a bad job, or for doing something wrong. He or she may feel guilty, or afraid of never being hired again.

No matter why a person is depressed, after a while he or she should be able to feel better. But sometimes that doesn't happen. The person just keeps feeling worse and worse. In that case, help is

Marriages that are usually quiet and loving can become tense when one of the partners is unemployed.

needed. Your parent or a family member should talk to a social worker or a doctor. If someone who is depressed talks to you about hurting himself or herself, get help right away.

Money Troubles

The most common problem that families face when a parent is out of work is not having enough money to meet regular expenses. For some families, this means not having the money for treats and outings, or for new clothes. For other families, it can mean not having enough money for a place to live or food to eat. In any family, there will be changes in the amount of money parents have to spend. The longer your parent is out of work, the worse the money problem will be. Some families keep money in the bank as savings, to help them through difficult times. Many families do not. Families without savings may have to borrow money in order to make ends meet.

People often fight about money. When a parent is out of work, fighting about money can be a big problem. Your parents may be very worried. If one parent was fired for doing something wrong on the job, the other parent may be very angry. Sometimes when people are worried they can't help arguing. It is the only thing that makes them feel better. But that can be very hard on the family. If the fighting goes on for a long time, the family may need help to work out their problems. If there is physical violence, the family should get help immediately. If one or both of your parents lose control and hurt you, or if you are afraid they might, get help. Do not wait. Go to a friend or neighbor, a minister or school counselor. They will understand. If you feel that you or someone else in your home is in danger because of a violent parent, call the police and get out.

Fear of the Future

Things might be difficult in the period just after a parent loses a job. But in a few months things usually begin to get back to normal. Still, between jobs everyone worries about what might happen if things don't get better. You and your parents will probably be afraid at times. What if there isn't enough money to pay the rent? Will you have to move to a different house, or a different town? Maybe you are worried that there won't be money for presents at Christmas. Maybe you are worried that there won't be enough money for food. It is normal to have these fears and doubts about the future. But there are ways to help no matter what happens. Remember, most of the time people find new jobs in only a few months. When you are afraid, it can help to talk to someone about your fears. If your parents seem too worried, try talking to a friend, or a guidance counselor. Someone who is a good listener will help you sort out your thoughts.

Moving to another home may be the only answer to solving the problems caused by the loss of a job.

Chapter 3

Long-Term Unemployment

In many cases, a person who is out of work finds a new job in a few weeks. Maybe it will take a month or two at longest. But not always. If your parent has been disabled, he or she may not be able to go back to work at all. Perhaps he or she will have to find a completely new kind of work. When people are laid off, they may have to find a different kind of work before they can get another job. In either case, your parent will have to get special training for a new job. If your parent was fired for doing a bad job, he or she may have a hard time getting a new job. There are many reasons that people do

27

not find work again right away. Whatever the reason, the longer your parent remains unemployed, the more difficult it will be for the whole family.

Moving

When a parent is out of work for a long time, the family may have to move. Sometimes the move is made to save money. Your family may have to move to a cheaper place. If you live in a house, you may have to move to an apartment. You may have to move to a different neighborhood, or a smaller house. Or you may have to move so that your parent can look for work in a new place. This is more likely if he or she wants to make a fresh start because things ended badly in the last job. If your parent was laid off, your family may have to move to a place where he or she can find the same kind of work.

Moving is hard. If you move very far away from your old home, you may feel lonely. You will probably miss your old friends and school. Try to remember that it is not your fault that your family is having hard times. If you must move, try to prepare yourself. Learn as much as you can about the place you'll be living before you get there. Find out what is interesting and special about it. And keep in touch with your old friends by writing them letters, or talking on the phone (if it's not too expensive). Moving has a good side, too. You will have the opportunity to experience a new place and to make new friends.

Becoming Homeless

Homelessness is a growing problem. There is not enough low-income housing for the people who need it. Most people who lose their jobs do not become homeless. But some do. If a parent, or both parents, are out of work for a very long time, it is possible that your family could lose its home. But there are places to seek help (see Chapter Six) and there are ways to avoid becoming homeless. It is important to seek help early.

Drug and Alcohol Abuse

When a parent is out of work for a long time, the stresses of being unemployed may become harder and harder to deal with. Your parent may try to relieve the stress by getting drunk, or using drugs. If your parent has lost a job because of a drug or alcohol problem, being out of work can make things worse. If this happens, your family will need professional help.

You cannot force your parent to change. You are not responsible for your parent's problem with drinking or drugs. But you *can* try to help *yourself.* There are people who can help you. And there are places your parent can go for help. You may find yourself thinking about using drugs or alcohol.

Your difficult family situation is stressful for you, too. Don't drink alcohol. Don't do drugs. There are much better ways to deal with stress—ways that will help to improve your life, not make it worse. (See Chapter Four and the Where to Go for Help section at the end of the book.)

Physical Violence/Sexual Abuse

If your parent cannot cope with being unemployed, he or she may become violent. Your dad may beat your mom. There may be fighting, yelling, and screaming in the house all the time. Your parent may hurt you or your brothers or sisters. That is abuse. If it happens, get help right away. Call the police. Hurting others is against the law.

If your parent begins acting strangely and abusively, he or she needs help. The fact that your parent is out of work is not your fault. You should not be punished for that in any way.

Sometimes a person who is very depressed does things to hurt other people. A parent who feels bad about himself or herself may do things that are strange or scary. That can happen if your parent develops a problem with drinking or drugs. Sometimes the abuse is not verbal or physical, but sexual. If your parent does anything to hurt you, get help—even if it makes your parent angry. You do not deserve to be treated badly. Remember that your parent needs help too. He or she will get help

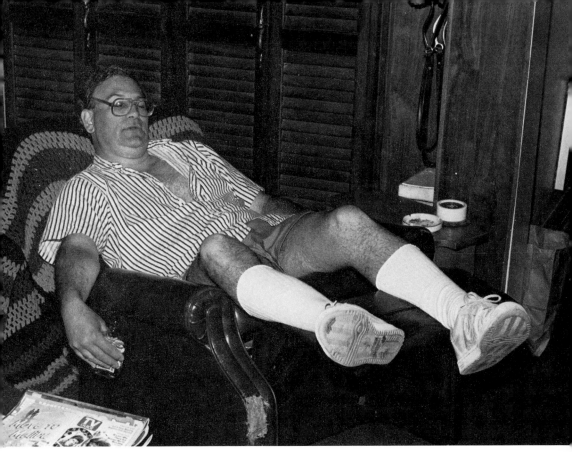

Depression is common among people who lose their jobs.
The abuse of alcohol or drugs can become problems
as well.

only if you let someone know what is going on.
Talk to a trusted friend or family member, or a
minister, or guidance counselor. Do not be afraid to
go to the police.

*Kareem's father was out of work for almost two
months when Kareem was thirteen. One day after
school he called a family meeting. Kareem and his
two sisters sat around the table with their mom and
dad.*

*"Kids," Kareem's mom said, "there is something
important we need to talk about."*

_"You know I've been looking for work," said
Kareem's dad. "Since the plant closed I haven't found
another job. But I think if I look somewhere else I
can find work._

_"Your mom and I are taking a trip down South.
We'll stay with my brother. Once I find a job, we'll
look for a house. Then we'll send for you."_

_Kareem's sisters looked upset. They were younger,
five and eight. "Who will take care of us?"_

_"You can stay with Grandma and Poppy. You can
get to school on the bus every day, just like you do
now," said their mom. "Kareem is going to stay with
Uncle Joe and Aunt Bess. Their house is near the
junior high."_

_"I know you kids will miss each other, and you'll
miss us, too," said Kareem's dad. "But it's just for a
little while. We'll miss you all. We'll all be together
again soon."_

Splitting Up the Family

If your parent is out of work for a long time, the
best thing for everyone may be for the family to
split up. This is a very hard choice to have to make,
but in some cases it is the best thing.

There are different reasons for splitting up the
family, and different ways for it to be done.

The family may split up so that one parent can
work in another place. Suppose your father can

find work in another state but doesn't want to up-root the whole family. Perhaps he will go alone to work until the family can afford to join him. Or he will work somewhere else until he can return to a job close by. Hopefully, such arrangements will be temporary. The family will be back together when the crisis is past.

If your parents can no longer afford a place to live, they may try to find a place for you and your brothers and sisters to live. They may send you to stay with your grandparents, or even with family friends. There are also government and state agencies that can help find a foster family for children whose parents cannot care for them. The children may stay with a foster family until the parents are back at work and able to support their family again.

Your parent may be dealing with being out of work by drinking or using drugs, or being abusive. If that happens, you may be placed in a foster home for your own safety.

In the Long Run

Many different things can happen when a parent is out of work for a long time. It is important to understand that some of the things that might happen are bad. That way you can do your best to be prepared. Always remember that you are not to blame for hard times in your family. There are ways that you can get help if you need it.

Working within a smaller budget is one way families cope with a loss of income.

Chapter 4

Coping as a Family

Many things can happen when a parent is out of work. Some of them are very bad. Many of them are hard to handle. A few of them can be good. But whatever happens to your family, there are some basic things you can do. These things will help you get through a stressful time together. There are also things to do to make special problems easier to cope with.

Living on a Budget

Making a budget is the best way to keep track of money. Your parents may already do this for the household. When money is tight, it is very important to keep track of how it is spent. Ask your

parents about the family budget. If they are willing
to talk with you about it (and not all parents will
be), you may find it very helpful. Knowing how
much money comes into the house each month and
what it must be spent on can help you. You will
understand the reason that changes must be made.

For instance, your family may have spent $600 a
month on food in the past. Maybe you all went out
to dinner, or had Chinese take out or pizza a few
times each month. Maybe you could have any
treats or special foods you wanted. But the new
food budget may allow only $300 a month to be
spent on food for the whole family. That may mean
no more dinners out. It may mean no more take-
out food and little or no junk food. Maybe you will
eat less meat. Of course, every family is different.
It isn't really a hardship not to be able to eat whatever you want. But it can be a strange and upsetting change. Understanding why may help you to
miss it less.

If you have an allowance or a job, you can make
up your own budget. If the family is having bad
money problems, your earnings may go toward
helping everyone. If you are able to keep and use
your own money for yourself, try to spend it care-
fully. You don't need a lot of money to keep a budget. In fact, the less you have, the more important
it is to be careful about how you spend it.

How to Make a Budget

Dawn's teacher recommended her for a regular baby-sitting job. Now she would have some money of her own. Her mom ran the house on a budget. The family managed well, even when Dawn's father was laid off. Dawn asked her mom to help her make a budget, too. That way she could save money for a CD player.

Dawn and her mom wrote down all the things Dawn wanted money for. Then they worked out how much she could spend on each (snacks, movies, tapes, video rentals, etc.) every week and still have some money left over to save.

Dawn was very careful about spending the money she earned. She was able to buy the CD player much sooner than she had planned. And she had learned a lot. She made a list of other things she'd like to have. Saving every week would make it easy for her to get the things she wanted.

To make a budget, first write down the amount of money you expect to have each month. This is your *income*. Next, make a note of any savings you might have in a piggy bank or a bank account. Now think about the things you spend money on. Write down all your daily expenses, like lunch at school, and bus fare. Next consider weekly and monthly expenses. Is there something special you want to save money for? New sneakers? A bike? Birthday

presents? Consider how much money you will
need for these things. Then look at your budget.

How much money do you have left over after your
regular expenses? The left-over money is called
your *disposable income.* You can plan to use that
and some of your savings for the special things you
want. Of course, that may mean you need to save
for a few weeks or months. You may want to put a
certain amount of money into your savings each
month. Saving for something big, like going to
college or buying a car, will take a long time.

Make up a budget. Then keep track of how you
actually spend your money for a whole month.
After a month you will see if you need to change
any of the ways you spend your money.

Family Budget - May
Amount

1. Rent / Mortgage
2. Telephone
3. Electricity
4. Fuel
5. Car payment
6. Gasoline
7. Food
8. Cleaning
9. Entertainment
10. Clothing
11. Doctor
12. Dentist
13. Other expenses
                                 Total:

Keeping Morale Up

Morale is the general feeling of a person or a group. When your parent is out of work, he or she may feel depressed. The rest of your family may feel sad and worried too. It is important to find ways to keep your own spirits up. You must all try to enjoy some good times together.

Families that talk openly and share their feelings usually get through a crisis better than families who do not talk to each other. Talking is an important way of keeping spirits up and staying close. Often, understanding a problem makes it less scary.

Each family has different ways of having fun. And families have different ways of celebrating the good things in life. Some families are very religious. Church functions can be a good place to enjoy friends and forget about the pressures at home. Prayer and worship services make many people feel more hopeful during trying times. Talking to a rabbi, or minister, or other clergyman can be very helpful too.

Just having fun together is good, too. Watch a movie on TV together and make some popcorn. Go for a walk in the park, and have a picnic. Visit the zoo, or a museum. Going window-shopping can be fun—if it doesn't make you upset that you can't spend any money. Work together around the house with a radio playing (if you can agree on the music to play). Read together, and discuss what you think about the books or articles you share. Even preparing meals can be a time to have fun. If you can keep a sense of humor in hard times, it helps a lot. Tell funny stories about your day. Try not to cut yourself off from friends and relatives. When a family has hard times, sometimes they stop seeing other people. But staying in touch with friends and relatives helps to keep a family in better spirits. Besides, friends and family may be able to help with some of the problems.

Relieving Stress

There are good and bad ways to relieve stress. The good ways usually make life a little easier, or easier to bear. The bad ways usually relieve stress for only a short time and often end up making things a lot worse.

Everyone in your family will probably be under some stress when a parent is out of work. Think about how the situation affects you. How does it make you feel? What does it make you worry about? How does it affect the way you get along with other family members? Think about these questions. Then try to find ways to ease the stress they are causing.

Many people find that exercise is a good way to relieve stress. You might try running, bicycling, doing aerobics, or playing a sport at school. Walking is good too.

Showing support as a family can often be a great help to a parent who is out of work.

Writing is another good way to deal with stress. Sometimes writing down your feelings helps you to see things more clearly. Keeping a diary can be a relaxing and interesting experience. Reading is also a good activity. Some people feel that reading a good book is the perfect way to take a break from the things that are bothering them in everyday life. Reading adventure stories, mysteries, science fiction, romance, and fantasy can be a good way to relax.

Talking is often a good way to relieve stress. Just having a good talk with a friend can make you feel a lot better. Talking about your problems and fears can also be helpful. You may want to talk with your parents, your friends, a guidance counselor at school, or even a radio dee-jay. If you have really serious problems, there are hotlines you can call to get answers to questions or to just talk out your troubles. Look in the phone book for these special numbers.

There are lots of other good ways to relieve stress, like playing music, or drawing. The activity should help you to feel better without completely blocking out your situation. And you shouldn't feel bad about taking a break from the stresses of your family life. Make sure you get enough sleep, and that you eat a balanced diet. These things will help a lot when you are under stress. They will help you to cope. Some of these activities might include other members of your family. You cannot lessen the stress that your parent or other family members feel. They will have to do that for themselves. But you can make suggestions. And if you are in good spirits that may help everyone feel better.

Some of the bad ways people try to lessen stress are by drinking too much alcohol, taking drugs, or fighting. Or they may shut themselves off from everything and everyone and try to pretend that nothing is wrong. None of these things lessen stress. All of them make it worse and may cause many other problems in a person's life.

Counseling

Sometimes, whether you find a good way to deal with stress or not, you will need help from someone else to get through hard times. Maybe you or your whole family will go to a counselor. You can get professional help when you need it. If you or a family member feels out of control, you should seek counseling. There are good places to get help in a crisis, even if you don't have very much money. Try contacting your clergyman, a local mental health service, or a city or state social service agency.

You cannot force another person to get this kind of help. But if you see that your parent or other family member is in need of help, you can suggest it. You can even provide the name of a counselor or clinic. Be sure to find help if you need it.

Many teens welcome an opportunity to help the family's finances by taking a part-time job.

Chapter 5

What You Can and Can't Do to Help

Yₒu can help the family when a parent is out of work. You may want to help ease some of the stress your family is feeling. You may want to help out by getting a part-time job. And you will want to give help and support to your parent while he or she is looking for a new job.

Getting a Part-Time Job

It is not up to you to support your whole family. But you may be able to help out by bringing in money from a part-time job. Of course, how much you can earn depends on your age and the kind of job you get. Most of the jobs available to teen-agers do not pay very much. Many offer minimum wage (the lowest pay allowed by law). If you have skills or experience (if you can type, or repair cars, for instance) you may be able to get a job for higher pay.

Some jobs are good training, or good experience for other work you may do in the future. You may develop a new interest. A part-time job can turn into an opportunity to learn about something you never thought you would enjoy.

Here are some typical jobs that are open to teen-agers: baby-sitter, mother's helper, waiter or waitress, fast-food server or cook, delivery boy or girl, housekeeper, lawn worker, snow shoveler, house sitter, typist, clerk, cashier, salesperson. Of course, there are many other jobs as well.

If you decide to get a job, remember to choose one that won't get in the way of your schoolwork. Spend some time thinking about the pros and cons (good and bad things) about any job you apply for. How many hours per week will you be expected to work? Will the work be physically tiring? Do you have the skills or the right personality to do the job? (If you can't stand kids, don't be a baby-sitter. If you don't like being ordered around, don't become a waiter.) Also, find out if your school has a work-study program. Such a program allows you to get school credit for working. Some schools will also help students find part-time work.

You might be able to help out the family by working part-time. You will certainly benefit from having a job of your own. But you probably won't be able to support your family. And no one should expect you to.

Sharing Household Chores

One of the best ways to help your family when your parent is out of work is to help around the house. There is always housework to be done. Offer to do some specific tasks on a regular basis. Agree to cook dinner on certain nights of the week, or do the laundry on Saturday morning. A family that works out such simple matters together often feels less stress over larger problems.

Helping with Your Parent's Job Search

Michael's mom had been out of work for over a month. She had worked in a factory for many years. The factory had closed down. Michael's mom wanted to work in an office. But she had no job skills for office work.

"We have career counseling at school," Michael told his mom. "They are teaching us to figure out what skills we have that can be used on a job. They are also teaching us how to look for a job.

"My counselor told me about a book that can help a person decide what kind of job to look for. They have it in the library at my school. I'll bring it home. We

can look at it together. It can probably help you de-
cide what kind of job to look for. And it will give me
some more ideas about what I could do after I finish
school this summer."

  The best thing you can do to help with your parent's job search is to believe in his or her ability to
get another job. Perhaps you may be able to talk to
your parent about finding a new job. You can look
through the want ads in the paper. You can help
your parent make a list of skills and goals. You can
even help your parent practice interviewing. All of
these things will help you, too, when you are ready
to be on your own. Knowing how to find a job, and
what kind of job you want to look for, will make the
task easier.

  There are many books about finding and getting a
job. You can read about how to interview for a job
and how to find a better job. You can help your
parent learn what skills he or she has. You can help
your parent learn new skills. You might want to
check some books out at the library and share one
or two with your parent.

  Letting your parent know that you are willing to
help out is important. Let her or him know you can
be counted on to make things easier when she or
he is back at work, too. It can be hard to get used
to new things. Help and support from family can
make a real difference in a positive way.

Helping with household tasks and cooperating with other members of the family lightens the burden for everyone during tough times.

Banks and other financial companies can offer loans to people who are dealing with unexpected problems.

Chapter 6

Getting Help for Special Problems

*L*uis *lives in New York with his mom and dad, three sisters, and two brothers. His father used to drive a taxi, but he has a problem with his back. He may never be able to drive a cab again. Luis's mom works, but she doesn't make enough to support the family. And there are doctor bills to pay, and hospital bills. The family needs help to stay together.*

Luis's dad cannot travel. His mom speaks only Spanish. So Luis must go with his mom to seek help. They will go to a social services office. They will learn how and where to seek help with medical problems and money problems. Luis's mom is happy that Luis can go with her. She will talk to him in Spanish, and he will explain things for her to the social worker.

The sort of help you need to deal with your parent's unemployment will depend on the problems the family is having. Each case is different. Once you know what your family's problems are, you can decide where to go for help.

It is not up to you to make your parent feel better, or to help him or her find a new job. For the most part, you can only help yourself. Of course, there are many ways that you can help your parents. But it is important to remember that the responsibility is theirs, not yours. They will have to take steps to work out their own problems. Your parent will feel much better when he or she sees that you are doing a good job managing your own responsibilities to yourself and keeping up with your schoolwork.

Questions about Fairness

There may be some questions about why your parent was fired. Today, in America, it is illegal for anyone to be fired because of their race, religion, handicap, or sex. It is also illegal to fire a woman because she is pregnant. If a person is fired for any of these reasons, it is a case of discrimination. It may be helpful to discuss these points with your parent. Does your parent think he or she might have been discriminated against? There are places to go for advice about discrimination. The Equal Opportunity Commission and other agencies— listed in the Where to Go for Help section of this book—can offer help with discrimination questions.

Financial Assistance

If your family has very bad money problems, you may want to seek help from state and local welfare agencies. Your family may want to apply for food stamps if you don't have enough money to buy groceries. Your parent may be eligible for some of the following:

- unemployment benefits
- disability insurance
- worker's compensation
- social security

These are all things that your parent must apply for. You cannot do it for him or her. Each case is different. Do you feel that your family is in need and your parent is unwilling or unable to get help? Call your state or local social services office. A social worker will put your family in touch with the right agencies. You will all get the help you need.

Emergencies

If you have an emergency situation (physical violence, sexual abuse, possible suicide) call the police, or the fire department, or even a neighbor who can help you. Call information for the right hotline number. Be sure to read through the list of agencies in the Where to Go for Help section of this book. If you feel that anyone in the family is in danger, get help right away. Keep telling people until someone agrees to help.

Developing job skills, getting an education, and taking good care of
yourself are the best ways to get ready for the future.

Chapter 7

Preparing for the Future

*D*onna's mom stood back for a moment, looking *again at Donna to make sure that her graduation gown was adjusted correctly over her clothes. The cap, with its tassel, was at just the right angle.*

Donna was happy to be graduating and glad that she had stayed in school. "Thanks, Mom, for making sure I didn't leave school. I'm glad I didn't quit to go to work when Dad was laid off. Now he's working again and I have a job, too—a good job. I'm sure I'm going to like working at the bank. And I think I'd like to go to college, too, after a while."

Your parent may go back to work soon. But what will happen if he or she is unemployed again? Are there ways to avoid the troubles you've been through? Yes and no.

How to Be Prepared

No one can be sure that he or she will never be out of work. There are things a family can do to be prepared. If possible, a family may keep money in a savings account, pension fund, or insurance policy. This money is to be used for emergencies only. A family with an emergency fund may have fewer problems when a parent is out of work.

Aside from having emergency money, a family can prepare for rough times by learning to work together. Learning how to get along well with each other will make a family better able to face hard times.

Career Counseling

Your parent's job problems might make you think about what sort of work you want to do in the future. Your parent might need help in deciding what sort of new job to look for. If your parent is thinking of trying something new, he or she is facing a challenge. Going to see a career counselor is probably a good idea. Your school guidance counselor may be able to give you advice about careers. Or you can ask your librarian for help in finding career counseling information.

Helping your family through hard times provides you with good experience. You will probably find it easier to get and keep a good job once you have finished school. And you will know what to do and how to get help if you are ever out of work.

Glossary—*Explaining New Words*

abuse Harm, hurting.

alcoholic Person addicted to alcohol.

budget Plan for spending money.

debt Owing something to someone.

depression Sadness, feeling of hopelessness.

disability Illness or injury that leaves a person unable to work.

discrimination Unfair treatment based on race, sex, religion, or handicap.

disposable income Money left over after paying for necessary expenses like food, rent, etc.

economize Save money by spending only what is absolutely necessary.

foster home Home where children may live temporarily when parents are unable to care for them.

income Money earned.

incompetence Inability to do a job.

insurance Contract that provides money in case of illness or injury.

lay off When workers lose their jobs due to an employer's problems, such as factory closings.

morale Spirit, feeling of a person or a group.

stress Pressure, strain.

strike Workers stop working, together, to force employers to make changes, like paying higher wages.

technology Scientific improvement of ways of making and doing things.

unemployment benefits Money paid to a person who loses a job, if not "fired for cause" (if it wasn't his or her fault).

union Organization of workers.

Where to Go for Help

You may have questions or concerns about the reason your parent was fired. You may want to know if help is available for your parent. Some of the following agencies may help. In addition, there are addresses for organizations that can help with alcohol and drug abuse problems, family violence, sexual abuse, and suicide prevention. You (or your parent) may also want to contact your State Employment Service and/or your State Labor Department. You can look them up in the blue pages in the back of your phone book.

You may want to write to some of these agencies. Many have free publications they will send you. Or they can direct you to other organizations that can give your family the kind of help you need.

United States Department of Labor
200 Constitution Avenue NW
Washington, DC 20210

National Labor Relations Board
1717 Pennsylvania Avenue NW
Room 701
Washington, DC 20570

Small Business Administration
1441 L Street, NW.
Washington, DC 20416

Rehabilitation Services Administration
330 C Street, S.W.
Washington, DC 20202

Equal Employment Opportunity Commission
1900 E Street, NW.
Washington, DC 20415

Handicapped Employment Program
200 Independence Avenue, S.W.
Washington, DC 20201

Office of Civil Rights
200 Independence Avenue, S.W.
Washington, DC 20201

Social Security Administration
6401 Security Boulevard
Baltimore, MD 21235

Federal Job Information Center
1900 E Street, NW.
Washington, DC 20415

Alcoholics Anonymous World Services
P.O. Box 459 Grand Central Station
468 Park Avenue South
New York, NY 10163

National Association of State Mental Health
  Program Directors
1001 Third Street SW
Suite 115
Washington, DC 20024

Families Anonymous
P.O. Box 528
14617 Victory Boulevard
Suite 1
Van Nuys, CA 91408

Drug and Alcohol Council
396 Alexander Street
Rochester, NY 14607

Children's Bureau Clearinghouse on Child Abuse
  and Neglect Information
Department of Health and Human Services
P.O. Box 1182
400 Sixth Street SW
Washington, DC 20013

For Further Reading

Miner, Jane Claypool. *Unemployment.* New York: Franklin Watts, 1983. This book discusses what it is like to be out of work and why so many people lose their jobs.

Howard, Richard D. *Unemployed Uglies.* Pendergrass Publishing, 1966. This book is about unemployed people.

Honigsberg, Peter J. *Unemployment Benefits Handbook.* Addison-Wesley, 1981. This book has a lot of information about benefits available to unemployed people.

Figler, Howard. *The Complete Job-Search Handbook.* New York: Henry Holt & Company, 1979. This book helps you to figure out what your skills are and how to put them to use to find a new job.

Check your local library for magazine articles on unemployment and other books on the subject. Ask your librarian to help you find them.

Index

63

About the Author
Stephanie St. Pierre has written more than twenty-five books for children
and young adults, and has been an editor and designer for more than
eight years. She currently lives in Brooklyn, New York, where she works
as a freelance editor and writer.

About the Editor
Evan Stark is a well-known sociologist, educator, and therapist—as well
as a popular lecturer on women's and children's health issues. Dr. Stark
was the Henry Rutgers Fellow at Rutgers University, and associate at the
Institution for Social and Policy Studies at Yale University, and a
Fulbright Fellow at the University of Essex. He is the author of many
publications in the field of family relations and is the father of four
children.

Acknowledgments and Photo Credits
Cover photo by Chuck Peterson
Photographs on pages 2,13,23,25,34,44,50,55: Barbara Kirk; page 8: Wide
World Photo; pages 18,21,31,41: Stuart Rabinowitz; page 49: Stephanie
FitzGerald.

Design/Production: Blackbirch Graphics, Inc.